Urban Church Planting

Urban Church Planting

Journey into a World of Depravity, Density, and Diversity

STEPHEN M. DAVIS
Foreword by John P. Davis

RESOURCE *Publications* • Eugene, Oregon

URBAN CHURCH PLANTING
Journey into a World of Depravity, Density, and Diversity

Copyright © 2019 Stephen M. Davis. All rights reserved. Except for brief quotations in critical publications or reviews, no part of this book may be reproduced in any manner without prior written permission from the publisher. Write: Permissions, Wipf and Stock Publishers, 199 W. 8th Ave., Suite 3, Eugene, OR 97401.

Scripture quotations are from the ESV® Bible (The Holy Bible, English Standard Version®), copyright © 2001 by Crossway, a publishing ministry of Good News Publishers. Used by permission. All rights reserved.

Resource Publications
An Imprint of Wipf and Stock Publishers
199 W. 8th Ave., Suite 3
Eugene, OR 97401

www.wipfandstock.com

PAPERBACK ISBN: 978-1-5326-9616-9
HARDCOVER ISBN: 978-1-5326-9617-6
EBOOK ISBN: 978-1-5326-9618-3

Manufactured in the U.S.A. 04/18/19

This book is dedicated to my family—
my wife Kathy who has faithfully served the Lord and followed her husband around the world for over forty years; my two sons, Andrew and Tim, who God gave us in a remarkable way and who have brought great joy into my life; my parents, James and Alberta Davis, now with the Lord and who I will see again, who loved me when I was unlovable and modeled Christ with grace and wisdom; and my brother John, who led me to Christ, and with whom I have had the privilege to serve the Lord at Grace Church Philly.

Contents

Foreword by John P. Davis	ix
Preface	xi
Introduction	xiii
1 | The City in the Bible	1
2 | What has Changed? What Remains the Same?	6
3 | From Paris to Philadelphia	12
4 | Leadership Dream Team that Wasn't	16
5 | Back to Prison	20
6 | Two Fundamental Questions	26
7 | Dangers of Cultural Accommodation	30
8 | Some Nuts and Bolts	35
9 | Why Some Church Planters Never Plant Churches	43
10 | Church and Kingdom in the City	48
Conclusion	57
Bibliography	61

Foreword

IN 1973 I HAD the joy of seeing my brother Steve come to Christ. The gospel immediately began a life-long work of compelling him to love and to serve His Lord and Savior. Together we have had the joy of growing in the gospel and partnering in church planting for over 40 years. As a seminary student Steve and his wife assisted and served in our church plant in Bucks County, PA. In the early 1980s our new church gladly partnered with his church plant in the Roxborough section of Philadelphia. Later we had the privilege of supporting him when he was called to church planting in France and Romania. Since 2009 we have had the opportunity to work together in planting a multi-ethnic church in Philadelphia.

As Steve points out, church planting does not always work out the way we plan. Early on we resisted having a 'target group.' We decided we would love and reach the people whom the Lord placed in our paths. In God's providence we moved from a university area of the city ministering to a mix of students, young professionals, and a diversity of neighbors to ministering in a largely Hispanic neighborhood with a church comprised mainly of Latino and African immigrants. Had we been committed to a 'target group' we might be living with disappointment, but instead we find great joy in loving and ministering to the people whom the Lord has given us.

Steve continues to be a faithful and wise church planter, avoiding the passing fads in church planting, retaining a high view of Scripture and the centrality of the gospel, and believing that establishing and strengthening the local church is still God's plan

FOREWORD

for making disciples of all nations. You will find his journey both entertaining, encouraging, and insightful. Be blessed and challenged as you read.

JOHN P. DAVIS, DMIN
LEAD PASTOR, GRACE CHURCH PHILLY

Preface

URBAN CHURCH PLANTING WILL be more challenging and more disappointing than you imagined. My intention is to neither over-glamorize urban church planting nor present a portrait of despair. There are no great church planters. After all, church planting is God's work. His work always succeeds. Yours may not. Or at least not be what you so carefully planned and strategized. The mention of depravity, density, and diversity in the title of this book does not suggest that these descriptors are limited to cities. However, you will often discover a greater concentration of these characteristics along with more crime and poverty than you might have experienced in your former world. For some, the urban church planting dream drifts into a nightmare.

    The culture shock of moving into and living in the city is every bit as real as someone moving overseas to learn how to navigate in a new culture and learn a new language. Learn a new language, really? Well, that might not always be true but if you church plant in Philly and come from another region of the country you will be noticed, and not always in a positive sense, with your Midwestern, Southern, or New England accent. I'm from Philly so I can turn the accent on if I need to (to my wife's chagrin). A few years ago, we had work done on our house and my wife was the only one home when the contractor came. He asked her in his mumbled Philly accent, "You're not from here, are you?" As believers, none of us are really from here since we've been born from above. Yet God has called us to serve him wherever that here may be at the time. We will always be strangers and outsiders in some ways. We are a pilgrim people on a journey. In the biblical storyline, what God began in the garden ends in the city, the New Jerusalem, which will be unlike any earthly city. In our day, God is not more interested in the city than other places. Yet in the city you are more likely to find the nations of the world gathered in a grand mosaic which reminds us that the people for whom Christ died come from every tribe, every language, and every people. If the city is where God has called you to minister, be aware of the challenges you will face, and be prepared to enter a world where you dare not walk alone. The city may not be safe but it is the safest place to be if God is with you.

Introduction

FOR OVER THIRTY-FIVE YEARS God has granted me the immense privilege to participate in planting churches in the United States and in Western and Eastern Europe. In addition, I have either travelled or taught throughout Europe, Asia, Africa, and South America. I was on a study trip in Israel in 1981 when Israel bombed the Iraqi nuclear reactor. I was church planting in Philadelphia in 1985 when the city bombed the MOVE enclave. I was in Yugoslavia in 1995 when NATO bombed Sarajevo and we made a mad dash for the Hungarian border. I was in China in 2002 during the SARS outbreak as we headed to Hong Kong and wondered why people were wearing masks. I was on my way to Beirut for a church dedication service in 2006 when Israel bombed Lebanon and I was stranded in Paris for a week (great place if you must be stranded). I have my experiences, many which I never sought but for which God had some purpose. As a result I have perspectives and I have opinions. These experiences are mine. They have been shared with my family. They may not be reproduced exactly in anyone's life. Yet they may serve in some way to better prepare others who sense God's calling in their lives to church planting. Now I am back in Philly and want to explain my church planting journey.

Our first church plant was in 1982 in Philadelphia. My wife and I were fresh out of seminary and in our late 20s when we first launched into urban church planting. That first church continues to exist with a different name and in a different location. I was young. I was inexperienced. I was impressed with my training. I made rookie mistakes. God gets the credit for whatever good came out of it. When my wife and I along with our two small children left for France in January 1988, we were young enough to still be naïve in some ways about expectations and soon realized that although we might have had a lot to offer we still had much to learn. We left the US for the mission field as heroes and arrived in France as idiots (in that we couldn't really function on our own). The benefit of going to France when we did in our early thirties after planting a church in Philly and seeing it continue under new leadership was that I knew something about the struggles and challenges of church planting. The problem was that I knew little to nothing about planting churches in France. Thankfully, we worked alongside a French pastor and his American wife whose eyes helped us begin to understand the culture. Our first French church-planting experience was in the city of Thionville in northeastern France as we began language study. From there we were sent to Laon, a small town which served as the administrative capital of the region of Aisne, France's capital over 1000 years ago. There we planted a new church which slowly developed over five years and continues as a testimony in that city to this day.

In 1989 with the fall of the Berlin Wall and the collapse of communism, ministry doors opened in Eastern Europe. After several visits to Romania to teach and for vacation, and after six-and-a-half years of life and ministry in France, we moved to Romania in the summer of 1994 to the city of Oradea. My wife cried when she knew we were leaving France. I discovered it was more because she would need to learn another language than anything else. She followed me faithfully. Our children were now old enough to know the difference in living standards. We initially had six-month visas. When it came time to renew them our youngest son, who thought we would be there for only six months, asked if we were going back to France. We weren't. Our sons adapted to a new life and new language. This time the ministry emphasis was on theological training for pastors who were denied the opportunity for formal study under communism. Our time in Romania, the joys and sorrows of ministry there, would require another book. Suffice to say that God gave us five marvelous years of ministry in facilitating

INTRODUCTION

church planting mostly in Romanian villages where paved roads, indoor plumbing, telephones, and other amenities that we took for granted were still in the future tense.

When we went to Romania we had a five-year plan with the intention of returning to France once trained national leadership was in place. We did not return to France, sensing no clear direction. In 1998 we returned to the United States to continue my studies and we were looking for the next step. As I was pursuing my doctoral studies at Trinity in Deerfield, IL, a large suburban church outside of Philadelphia with which I had been connected for years invited me to join the staff as director of domestic church planting and overseas ministries. We relocated from Illinois to Pennsylvania and served in this capacity until 2009. During that time, from 2006–2008 my wife Kathy and I split our time between Paris, France and Pennsylvania. It was a good gig. Our youngest son was still in college. He left for college in the fall. We left for France. He returned to Pennsylvania for holiday and summer breaks. We returned to be with him. Those two years in France gave my wife the opportunity to travel with me to Spain, Lebanon, and China for teaching and to visit missionaries. We knew that ultimately we would need to decide between France or the United States. As much as we loved what we were doing it was grueling at times and there was something missing due to our inability to have ministry continuity.

The second chapter of this book will continue the story and how we left Paris to eventually return to Philadelphia. It will also help to explain the purpose of this book. Simply put, this is my journey, one I could not have made without God and my wife. By the way, for men reading this book, make sure your wife is on board, not as a reluctant woman following her man and guilted into following you, but committed and content to live and serve in the city. Through this account, I would hope that others might gain insight into what ministry looks like, particularly urban church planting. I do not expect that your journey will be the same. What I hope you see is that in stepping into church planting you are stepping into the unknown, but you serve the All-Knowing One. He

Introduction

has always been faithful. All your plans, expectations, and dreams will not be accomplished. You will at times alternate between joy and sorrow, between grateful and begrudging ministry, between delight and despair, and between encouragement and disappointment in yourself and in others.

There are many things you will need to serve God faithfully—a strong sense of his sovereignty, a commitment to the gospel, a supportive family, and a sense of humor. You will find more on that in other books. You will also find elsewhere more on the steps to plant a successful church—core group, financial support, meeting place, and strategic planning. These are important. There is no formula, however, for church planting, no steps or principles that will guarantee success as many define it. That does not mean you should be unconcerned about steps and principles. You may see failure where God sees success. You might see success where God sees failure.

In the end, God calls us to faithfully live out the gospel, make disciples, and represent him well in our world. Our prayer is that this would lead to faithful, planted churches in God's time as a light in the community. Yet we do well to adjust our ambitions in surrender to God's sustaining grace whether or not the results pass muster in the eyes of others. God is concerned about sinners coming to a saving knowledge of Christ, following his Son in believer's baptism, and being incorporated in a body of believers. God is also faithful and will accomplish his purposes. Our part is to remain faithful, when all's going well, when all's going to, you know, the other place.

The first few chapters are mostly a recounting of events and people surrounding the urban church planting initiative in Philadelphia and the early years with its challenges. If you endure and read further I try to identify some particulars that might help in preparing for urban ministry. There are auras to be removed and struggles to be faced. I want to be as forthright as possible. Urban church planting is not God's calling or will for everyone who thinks about it, who aspires to it, who prepares for it, or who engages in it. Urban ministry is not more important than suburban

INTRODUCTION

or rural ministry. Yet urban ministry has some unique challenges and requires special gifting and preparation. This is especially so if all you have known is suburban or rural ministry. I hope this book provides doses of realism. I hope it also provides encouragement. Jesus promised he would build his Church. He uses means and men and women to accomplish that task. Yet we must never think that we, in our own strength and abilities, are actually doing what he alone can do. We are co-laborers with him.

So, this is my journey, with God, with my family, and with others in ministry. I don't know when this journey will end. I want to end well. I've seen far too many disqualify themselves from ministry for moral failure or doctrinal aberrations. While working on this book a high-profile evangelical pastor and his wife announced their divorce on separate Instagram accounts. Shortly after, he announced that he was no longer a Christian and was undergoing the deconstruction of a biblical worldview. He apologized for past positions he took on biblical sexual ethics and his previous opposition to so-called marriage equality. He now affirms what God condemns. The tragedy is that apostates rarely leave quietly and now have social media to revel in their newfound freedom and influence others to follow them in making a shipwreck of their faith. I've seen many leave the ministry for other reasons. Some needed to leave or maybe never should have been in ministry in the first place. No one is immune or invincible. Don't believe for a moment that you are. You will need people in your life to encourage you and hold you accountable. You will need a genuine walk with Christ and a firm, ongoing belief in the power of the gospel to save and keep you from falling. The journey has been far different in some ways than what I envisioned, mostly better, sometimes more difficult, more heartbreaking, and more puzzling than I imagined. I do know where the journey will end, with God, with my family, and with God's people forever in his presence. There are things I've learned, unlearned or still need to learn along the way. There are challenges and struggles. This is about still learning contentment and seeking satisfaction in God when discontent and unsatisfied. This is my story in God's story.

Chapter 1

The City in the Bible

It's been said that in the Bible life begins in a garden and ends in a city, the New Jerusalem. In between the Garden of Eden and the Eternal City we see the importance of cities as centers of God's purposes. Jonah was called to preach in and against Nineveh "that great city" (Jonah 1:2). Did you ever imagine what might've happened if he had stayed in Nineveh after multitudes repented rather than leaving the city to sulk and wait for its destruction? The Hebrew word for "city" occurs over 1,000 times in the Old Testament. The Greek word occurs over 150 times in the New Testament. More than 140 cities are mentioned in the Bible. When you read the book of Acts you are struck by Paul's strategy for planting churches in major population centers, going from city to city. You soon realize that the New Testament "was quite purposefully written within a missionary context, and that particular context was mostly urban."[1]

Augustine said there were two cities in every city in which the citizens serve different masters and live by different standards. For centuries cities were centers for gospel ministry with the gospel going out from cities to the surrounding regions, towns and villages. Cities remain the places of greatest influence and, with

1. Ortiz, "Church and City," 46.

their dense and diverse populations, the places of greatest need with their depravity. However, we have witnessed a phenomenon in this past generation of de-churching in the cities in North America. In many regions of our nation, the majority of Christians are now suburban and rural. Our world is becoming increasingly urbanized at the same time many cities are becoming de-Christianized. It's not that there are no churches in cities but that there are comparatively few relative to the number of inhabitants. And often those churches which remain do not have the resources for ministry since those resources fled to the suburbs with those who possessed them.

In our cities today we find the nations of the world but fewer and fewer Christians.[2] In our nation's cities, including Philadelphia, we find the centers of political power, universities and world-class hospitals. But once again we find fewer and fewer Christians. If we are to have an impact in our society today we must take seriously church planting in urban areas. With the flight from cities across our country in the past few decades, we have witnessed the rise of suburban megachurches. Many of these churches were built largely, although not exclusively, with Christians who fled the cities for a better life—defined as more space, more safety, less noise, better schools, and fewer people. Of course with suburbanization we find many of the ills and inconveniences once associated with city living now in the suburbs. As a result many people are pushing out further to get away from other people. One Christian told me he wanted to live in a place where he had no neighbors but acres of ground to guarantee his privacy. That way of thinking is contrary to Scripture. It's understandable that many people fled the cities. There was no will to stay when conditions deteriorated and new-found prosperity enabled upward mobility. It's tragic that much of that was done to escape from people who were different than us. What's done is done. It is not excusable, however, to have abandoned dense population centers if it was in order to fulfill our purposes and neglect God's. We exist to fulfill His purposes. For some that means a return to the city. There are encouraging signs

2. Bergquist and Crane, Review of *City Shaped Churches*, 199.

today that more and more of God's people are answering the call to return to the city knowing full well that the challenges confronted can only be met by Almighty God. It's not for everyone but it is certainly for some, perhaps for some of you.

When we moved back into the city in 2009 we were reminded daily of the challenges people face each day. Our move back to Philadelphia presented additional challenges for us in downsizing from a house into an apartment. It's amazing how much needless stuff you acquire over the years and it was somewhat freeing to get rid of stuff we really didn't need and that others could use. One of the responses we often received from people about moving back into the city to plant a church was, "That sounds exciting!" I wasn't sure how to respond. "Exciting" is not one of the words I'd use to describe this ministry move. I think I would use words like "wearying," "draining," or "challenging." When I was writing this chapter, I took a lunch break with my wife. We walked down to the corner to see police action a couple blocks away with two news helicopters hovering overhead. We later discovered that a police pursuit ended with the suspects' car crashing into six other vehicles. A few days later my brother and I were meeting to look at a rental location and passed several police officers talking outside a coffee shop on Lancaster Avenue. A few minutes later they were running to their cars with sirens blazing. Maybe that's what people mean by exciting.

There are daily reminders that city life is not a choice easily made. We did not choose to return to Philadelphia because it would be the most fun place to live, the safest place to live, the least expensive place to live, or where we could find the most square footage for our money. If life is about square feet of living space then we have the wrong priorities anyway. I recognize that city living is not for everyone and that churches are needed everywhere there are people. I remember waiting outside a Chinese take-out for my order and sitting down on a step next to a homeless man. In those few minutes I was able to hear his story and tell him the good news of God's love revealed in Christ Jesus. One of my sons was with me and I told him that this was one reason I wanted to be back in the city. He looked at me slightly puzzled and I said that being in the city I am reminded more often of the ravages of sin and the plight of those living in the streets. One writer observes that "almost everyone residing in poor inner-city neighborhoods is struggling financially and therefore feels a certain distance from the rest of America."[3] It's not that there are no homeless people or poverty to be found in the suburbs. But they are often better hidden and are easier to escape in suburban developments. Many urban areas have undergone enormous economic changes due to deindustrialization and rapid technological changes which "led to a steady loss of the unskilled and semiskilled manufacturing jobs that, with mixed results, had sustained the urban working class since the start of the industrial revolution."[4]

I wasn't looking for confirmation that God wanted us in the city but it is encouraging when God gives you a glimpse of what he is doing. A few weeks before moving back into the city I was standing in my garage in suburban Philadelphia going through stuff and packing. My cellphone rang and my brother John told me that someone wanted to speak with me. An unfamiliar voice on the other end asked me if I remembered a guy named Pete who used to hang out at a recreation center in Philadelphia years ago. It turned out that John had been talking to Pete, who lived on the same block, and had told Pete that about growing up in the Olney-Feltonville section of the city. John gave him a business card and when Pete saw "Davis" he asked John if he knew a "Stevie" Davis. John told him that we were brothers and Pete proceeded to explain how I messed him up years ago. You see Pete used to buy bags of heroin from me. He recalled the day he came to my house and I told him I wasn't dealing drugs anymore because I found Jesus. I stood in my garage and cried as I was reminded once again how good God had been to me in saving me from early death and certain hell and had now given me this opportunity to meet again someone like Pete and tell him what great things God had done for me. The following day I met Pete and had that opportunity.

3. Anderson, *Code of the Street*, 35.
4. Anderson, *Code of the Street*, 108.

Pete made a profession of faith and for several months attended services at our new church before moving out of the area.

In Jeremiah 29:7, Jeremiah called on the people in exile to seek the welfare (shalom) of the city. That remains our desire for Philadelphia and other urban centers. And the best way to do that is by making Christ known and planting new churches. We have no idea what God will do yet our confidence is in him and in his Word. We yearn to see the gospel of God's grace continue to transform the lives of those enslaved in sin and see churches planted in the great and needy cities of our nation.

Chapter 2

What has Changed?
What Remains the Same?

IN 1982 MY WIFE and I planted our first church in Philadelphia—Faith Independent Baptist Church. For me it was a return to the city of my birth. For my wife it was an introduction to urban living. As a church we were known more for what we were against than for who we were or what we believed. I was the product of eight years of training and influences of those who discipled me. My heart was in the right place. I wanted to serve God and see people come to Christ. I was a happy separatist but others around me were probably less happy at times with my demeanor and stands on issues. Despite my immaturity, God blessed those years and a new church was planted which became self-supporting in a short time. After planting the church in Philadelphia from 1982–1987 my family went to France in 1988 and then to Romania in 1994 to engage in church planting and pastoral training ministry. Those years spent overseas provided opportunities for fellowship with believers from different horizons and spared me the need to engage in many of the needless conflicts being fought in the States. There was less need to conform to others' expectations of what it meant to be safely within the fundamentalist orbit. During that time overseas, I pursued further studies with Reformed Theological Seminary's extension in

Budapest and in time completed a master's degree in theological studies. For the first time I was challenged from a different theological perspective by men with whom I had strong disagreements. Yet I was persuaded of their evangelical commitment, their love for God, and their commitment to God's authoritative Word. I began to see that we could differ interpretatively in some areas and still enjoy fellowship in the gospel. However, I need to add an important proviso. Fellowship in the gospel does not necessarily lead to partnership in gospel endeavors. In order to plant a church together there needs to be greater agreement on doctrine and practice. For example, I am persuaded that Scripture teaches believer's baptism by immersion following conversion. I can fellowship with evangelical pedobaptists. I would not enter into a church planting partnership with them. That is my conviction and I don't pretend that everyone will agree with my position. Church planters working as a team need to set parameters for doctrinal and practical agreement and adopt a confession of faith before undertaking a church plant that might implode early on due to differences.

Back to the story. In late 1998 we returned to the States where I began a short residency in Deerfield, IL at Trinity Evangelical Divinity School and where I completed a DMin in Missiology in 2004 under the late Drs. David Hesselgrave and Paul Hiebert among others. Once again, I was struck by the combination of scholarship and godliness among the professors. There were differences in some areas, but the centrality of the gospel transcended those differences. From 1999–2009, I was missions pastor and director of church planting at a large, influential suburban church. I travelled frequently and taught overseas in Russia, Ukraine, Lebanon, Peru, China, South Africa and several other countries. There were opportunities to teach courses on missions and church planting at several schools and seminaries and invitations to preach at various conferences. My visits to China were especially revealing as we looked for house church leaders with whom we could partner for training purposes. I found myself looking for "significant compatibility" and agreement with the historic Christian faith rather than agreement with my all my convictions and preferences. A greatly expanded and fruitful teaching ministry continues in China today.

When we returned to the US from Romania in 1998 I knew that both I and the spiritual landscape that I had known had changed. Then in 2008, while temporarily living in France and helping to plant a new non-Baptist church in the Paris suburbs, for which I received some criticism, I wrote an opinion article on Fundamentalism. It was my way of signaling at that time that although I was on a journey out of Fundamentalism as I had known it, I wanted to remain friends with Fundamentalists. I began to write, to challenge conventions and traditions. I was not intentionally mean-spirited, but I was not always irenic and did not avoid controversy. When I described myself as a "soft cessationist,"[1] questioned elements of dispensationalism,[2] took issue with unbiblical separation,[3] did not unequivocally espouse Young Earth Creationism,[4] expressed my

---

1. I believe that God's Word as found in the 66 books of the Bible is the Church's final and inerrant authority for faith and practice. I do not believe that there are prophets or apostles in our day and reject any position that adds to divine revelation including the health and wealth false gospel. Yet in pioneer missionary situations where there is no Scripture available I do believe God might work in ways analogous to first century times. That is, I do not believe God speaks apart from Scripture where Scripture is accessible. Once Scripture has penetrated a culture/people, there is no longer a need for God to communicate through any medium besides Scripture.

2. It seems to me that promises made to Israel are fulfilled first in Jesus, the only sinless Israelite, then in the church, not as a replacement for Israel or restored Israel but as an expansion of the promises to include Jew and Gentile in one body, one people of God, one new humanity. One example would be the promise to Abraham for the land which has been expanded to the world (Rom 4:13).

3. One measure of our understanding of biblical separation may not be how quickly and how often and from how many we will separate, but with how many we will agree to walk together in true obedience and genuine fellowship despite our disagreements (Amos 3:3).

4. While the Bible does not claim to be a scientific textbook, when and where it speaks the Bible speaks with God's authority. That authority extends to the veracity of the Genesis account of divine creation whether in the recent or distant past including the historicity of Adam and Eve and the Fall. That authority does not extend to interpretations of the creation event and methodology used for determining the age of the earth. There is no contradiction

dismay at the paucity of resources committed to church planting, or challenged traditional thinking in the church's engagement with culture, I found more criticism than interaction. The criticism was not about the gospel. It was mostly about culture, tradition, and even personalities who thought I was out of line and should have kept a lower profile. Whether or not I should have written some of those articles for publication is another story although I have few regrets. I know there are some who possessed greater certainty in areas where I had questions. I know others who did not want to rock the boat and preferred to fly under the radar. I suppose that would have been a safer route for me, but that bridge had already been crossed. I must confess that I found somewhat amusing the wide range of men who disagreed with me, attacked me, or separated from me. There has been something for many to dislike although certainly not the same things.

Some might find it surprising that personal ministry experiences and exposure to other cultures have influenced me to such a degree. Our experiences or lack of them have a great part to play in how we read Scripture. We read it with the eyes of those around us, those who trained us, and those to whom we look for guidance. Our experiences should not determine our theology yet how we read and understand Scripture cannot be separated from our outside influences and experiences. Some may consider it a badge of honor to hold the same beliefs and convictions they held decades ago. While I remain absolutely and unapologetically committed to the fundamentals of the faith, I must confess that second and third-level commitments and interpretations are no longer a cause for separation or hindrance to fellowship in the gospel. Perhaps it is partly because I recognize it is God's work not mine and that I labor in his vineyard not one of my creation.

The time eventually came for me to seek to identify with men and movements which demonstrated greater generosity with dissent and challenge than I had found in my experience, to identify with those interested in productive gospel-centered,

---

between true science and theology but there are enigmas and unanswered questions, at least for me.

church-planting partnerships, and God willing, to seek teaching opportunities to train others for next generation church planting. I had no illusions that moving on would bring greater resources or guarantee success in church planting. I was not looking for greener grass. At that point any grass would do. To this day, I still welcome friendship and even partnership with my brothers in other movements who have not drawn unreasonable lines in the sand. I'm thankful for friendships which have lasted for decades. But I am too old to jump through all the hoops, too ornery to kowtow, and prefer relative obscurity and a few warm relationships to playing ingratiating politics and pleasing men.

Fast forward to 2019 where in that same city of Philadelphia I am now working with a team of elders since 2010 to plant another church in Philadelphia. The team includes my brother John who led me to Christ in 1973. Much has changed. Most remains the same. I would venture to add that what is essential has not changed in my view of the sufficiency of Scripture and my commitment to the preaching of the gospel. Over thirty-five years of ministry, study, relationships, and experiences have all conspired to bring me to the place I am today. I claim no special expertise, offer no guarantees of success, and sense an even greater dependency upon the Lord to build his church. Similar struggles, resistance to the gospel, and dependence upon Christ to build his church remain. New battles are being fought in the political and theological arenas. Partisan politics and opposition to scriptural teaching on marriage and sexuality have invaded churches to a degree never seen in my lifetime. Marriage has been redefined by the Supreme Court and many denominations promote a godless agenda which includes abortion and same-sex marriage. Happily our confidence is not in politics and we are not looking for a political solution to our nation's ills. We trust in a sovereign God who will bring all things to his desired end. We are not prepared to compromise what we believe and hold firm in order to accommodate or capitulate to a godless culture.

Amid this chaos and upheaval, we seek to plant a church faithful to the Word of God. We gather to worship the Triune God.

What has Changed? What Remains the Same?

We believe we can best bless our city in preaching and teaching God's Word. We are non-political and uphold biblical teaching on marriage and sexuality. We are a welcoming church. We love people and want to see them come to Christ. We would not be considered an affirming church in that we won't affirm all lifestyle choices and won't support the multiple agendas and social experimentation undermining the authority of Scripture. This nine-year-old church is ethnically, educationally, and economically diverse. We were given a church building by a church that closed its doors. The church gathers in my old neighborhood which has greatly changed since I lived there in the 70s, from a majority white working-class community to a majority immigrant neighborhood. Yes, much has changed over the years, but God has not. He is faithful and he remains the Lord of the harvest in these challenging and needy times, the ultimate Judge who knows the hearts, and the Accomplisher of his divine purposes. We preach Christ crucified, foolishness to many, but the power of God to those who believe.

Chapter 3

From Paris to Philadelphia

Paris is beautiful in springtime. The cherry trees in bloom on Les Champs Élysées. The Eiffel Tower bathed in evening light. April 2008 was a turning point in our lives and set my wife Kathy and me in a direction that would eventually bring us back to church planting in Philadelphia over twenty years after our first church plant there. It is amazing how many friends you have who want to visit when you live in Paris. But we always welcomed family. My brother John and his wife Dawn were visiting us at the time. We had a fabulous multi-course traditional French meal over several hours. Around midnight we wandered around the Champ de Mars, a large open space of grass with gardens extending from the Eiffel Tower to the École Militaire. The Eiffel Tower was aglow and there was something magical and romantic in the air. However, my brother and I took a bench and began to talk about ministry. Our wives took another bench and talked about whatever wives talk about. We thought they were talking about us but apparently they had other things to talk about than their husbands. John and I began to imagine what it might look like to return to Philadelphia and work together to plant a church.

Way back in 1978 my wife and I were involved for four years in a church John was planting in the Philadelphia suburbs while

I worked on my MDiv in seminary. Our backgrounds had been similar in our rebellion against God, dropping out of high school, fighting, experimenting with illicit drugs, criminal activities, frequent arrests, and general disdain for authority. Our conversions were also similar. Our dad led John to Christ in 1970. John led me to Christ in 1973. We both went to Bob Jones University and we have often said tongue-in-cheek that when we became Christians we needed to either go to jail or into the military. At Bob Jones we got both. In reality, it was exactly what we needed with a healthy dose of discipline and discipleship. They were formative years in our Christian lives for which we remain grateful.

John and I competed in some areas. In sports John was a better quarterback. I was a better receiver. He had a better outside shot in basketball. I was better under the boards. These days we no longer play many contact sports. We used to argue about who had more hair. We both went bald. Academically, we both pursued and obtained an MDiv at Calvary Baptist Seminary. I received mine first. Over time John continued his studies at Westminster Theological Seminary (ThM) and Biblical Theological Seminary (DMin). He received his DMin first and called me to let me know. I studied at Reformed Theological Seminary (MATS) and Trinity Evangelical Divinity School (DMin in Missiology) and earned a PhD in Intercultural Studies at the age of 64. Both of us consider that we are educated beyond our intelligence but immensely grateful that God restored our minds after ingesting, smoking, snorting, and mainlining substances that God never intended for those uses.

Over the years we had been in ministry in different places and, frankly, had some divergences and disagreements. We had both been staunch independent, fundamental Baptists and planted independent Baptist churches. It was all we knew at the time. It was an important part of our journey as young Christians and times that we look back on as foundational in our lives. The solid doctrinal foundation we received, the commitment to the supreme authority of God's Word, and confidence in the power of the gospel remain inculcated in our hearts and minds. I cannot speak for John, but I suspect his journey out of fundamentalism was influenced by his study of hermeneutics and as a student of Scripture he saw the need to allow God to change his heart and mind. For me, living overseas for over a decade in France and Romania gave me the freedom to think, study, and interact with believers in different cultural contexts and gave me perspectives that pushed me to move on from the militant separation of cultural fundamentalism while retaining a firm conviction in the fundamentals of the faith.

At the time of our conversation in Paris, John was pastoring a church he planted in Queens, New York. My wife and I were facilitating a church plant in the Paris suburbs and helping a church in Paris with an interim pastor. The suburban Paris church had French leadership and although we loved being part of the new church plant, we sensed that we were wanted but not necessarily needed. As John and I imagined ministry scenarios, we committed to think and pray about Philadelphia. We talked about how when we were young we were trouble in the city and now might be the time to return and do good in our "latter" years. We had contributed to the crime and decay in our own North Philly neighborhood with little concern for the community. John and his wife returned to the United States and we remained in France. The seed was sown and needed time to grow.

Kathy and I returned to the States shortly after and I resumed my position at a church in suburban Philadelphia. There was a debate going on in my heart and mind about how and where to best invest my life, or what was left of it at the ripe age of fifty-four. My position at that time was secure. I could travel freely to visit missionaries and to teach pastors in several countries. Of particular interest to me were China and Lebanon where the Lord had allowed me to spearhead ministry which brought great satisfaction. However, after ten years of international travel, normally with other pastors, rarely with my wife, and after two years in Paris with my wife, I did not relish a return to the former situation of leaving my wife behind. The church where I served was doctrinally sound yet I came to the point where I knew it was time to leave and pursue other ministry, hopefully with the church's support and blessing. We received the blessing but little support. After one year back in the States and now fifty-five, the time came for ministry change. Over that previous year my brother and I had met several times. We had been praying, dreaming, wondering if this was the time. And if it was the time, what was the plan?

Chapter 4

Leadership Dream Team that Wasn't

URBAN CHURCH PLANTING RAISES great enthusiasm, at least early on. As I began to share the vision for church planting with my suburban church's leadership and congregation, we received the church's blessing but not a place in the budget. The church had a seminary at the time and there were videos created to give the impression that the church was on the threshold of investing in urban church planting. The church had a wonderful history of church planting but limited effort in urban church planting in the city that was less than an hour away. And sad to say, little church planting of any kind today. Thankfully there was one generous church member who helped finance our move into the city and a partial salary. She gave the money to the church so there was at least the appearance that the church was supporting us. Once we left, we were out of sight and out of mind. You may read between the lines my disappointment in a church with which I had been associated for over thirty years. It was easy to remind myself that I had raised hundreds of thousands of dollars for the church's missionary endeavors and for the seminary. It was also necessary to remind myself that it was never my money to begin with and that human disappointment is a fact of life and ministry. You never really get over it. God gets you through it.

Leadership Dream Team that Wasn't

Now the time of planning had arrived. Through various contacts and friendships, a core of men emerged who caught the vision for urban church planting. Besides my brother and me, there were initially three other men and their families which gave us a leadership core of about fifteen people, adults and children. In addition to them, there were several families and individuals, including our sons, that although they did not intend to move into the city, wanted to be a part of the church plant to help it off the ground. The prospective leadership team met regularly. The men travelled often into the city seeking to determine where to locate the church plant. We met with other pastors in Philadelphia to get a sense of where churches were needed without stepping over each other and settled on University City in West Philadelphia. More specifically we decided to concentrate north of Market Street in the neighborhoods of Powelton, Mantua, and Belmont. The leadership team met to discuss books we were reading on urban ministry. The families gathered occasionally for picnics in order to get to know each other better.

One matter needed to be determined from the beginning. We already determined that we in the leadership team would all be elders. At the same time, we recognized that one elder would be "first among equals." With five men, each uniquely gifted, each with an ego, and each with ambition, who would be the lead pastor? Sometimes the answer may be obvious. It was in our case, not only to me with my biases, but to the others at the time. Of the five men in leadership, four of us had advanced theological training, three with an MDiv, one with an MA in Theology. Of those four two had professional doctorates (DMin). The education component was not in itself determinative yet weighed heavily in our thinking. My brother John and I were the ones with doctorates. His experience spanning several decades was a combination of church planting and pastoring. My experience was mostly church planting, both domestic and international. John had more pastoral experience, was a better expositor than all of us, and our selection of him as lead pastor was uncontested. With this decided we were ready to take some next steps.

17

John and his wife moved into Philadelphia in July 2009 followed by my wife and me later that year in October. Early on, John began looking for a suitable rental location in the area of the city we had settled on in West Philly. We found an afternoon rental at an Episcopal church and began meeting bi-weekly for several months before launching in March 2010. Our launch was simple. We did not want a huge launch with visitors from other churches to swell the attendance only to return to a small group the following week. The church attracted mostly students from surrounding universities and new move-ins from other states and countries. Very few people from the neighborhood showed any interest despite canvassing the community and holding outreach events. In a short time, the church's attendance averaged between 50–60 with spurts to 70–80 at times. We met Sunday afternoons simply because we couldn't find a morning location. After every service we had a meal which was a great time of fellowship but a lot of work, mostly for the elders' wives. The church was intentionally diverse—ethnically, economically, and educationally. John and I would kid people in saying that if everyone in the church looked like us, we would be disappointed. Those early months were greatly encouraging, and we saw God at work in lives.

The initial elder team did not last. One prospective suburban elder came during the pre-launch period but faded away once we began to meet regularly. They were a great couple, but I don't think they were ready to leave their established church and they had no desire to move into the city. Another elder left after about a year, partly disgruntled, partly disengaged and his original plan to move into the city never materialized. They were a great family and are serving the Lord elsewhere. Another couple with several children was enthusiastic about planting the church and planned to move into the city. They never made the move and over time, with other complications, they withdrew from the church and the couple eventually separated. They were a lovely family. The husband was gifted in speaking, writing, and in organizing events. This was heartbreaking for us. One of the great disappointments of ministry.

Early in the life of the church we had a visit from a man who saw one of our posters. He and his wife were in a Lutheran church. He came by himself to check us out to see if we were safe. His wife was afraid we might be a cult. I understand that if she had seen my brother's and my photos. This man was a Caucasian transplant from Pittsburgh. His wife was African American. They had met at the Lutheran church years before, married, had two children, and lived in a challenging neighborhood. They continued to attend their church in the morning and began attending Grace Church in the afternoon. They came to the point where they knew they needed to leave their church where they had been for many years and unite with a faithful, Bible-teaching church. The husband eventually became an elder and they have both served faithfully and generously. They were and are one of the highlights and joys of the ministry.

So, the dream team never came together. We had other promising elders along the way. One left the city and moved out of state. His wife never really adapted to city life. Another one was called, trained, and engaged in ministry, then concluded that he was not really called to ministry. He left the church, moved away, took a job, and now attends another church where he is serving the Lord. A third elder was disciplined for immorality, left the church, and was promptly accepted into membership by another church which never contacted us. Yet the Lord had his own team in mind. Today it's a team that includes a Kenyan, a Cameroonian, a Dominican, and a few old white guys. It might not be a dream team but it's not a nightmare either and has provided ministry opportunities abroad that we never imagined.

Chapter 5

Back to Prison

ONE MAJOR REASON FOR moving back into Philadelphia rather than staying in Paris was to invest in church planting in the city where frankly my brother and I had been hell raisers. Some people thought my wife and I were crazy to choose Philly over Paris (and sometimes I think they were right). John and I had both been involved in the drug culture of the late 60s and early 70s, had both dropped out of Olney High School, then had both become born again Christians, him in 1970, me in 1973. We both then went to college and graduate school and by God's grace have been in ministry for several decades in different places. With our children grown and out of the house it seemed like a good time to move back into Philadelphia and do there what we believed to be the greatest good—tell people about Jesus! We had no idea what God might do, had no place to meet, and no congregation. We had raised enough money for one of us to be supported fulltime in church planting and, as I said earlier, John seemed like the one better equipped and with more experience for that task. I started looking for work. I believe God opened the door to work with drug addicts in the prison system. I still had some street smarts. I had past acquaintance with illicit substances. I saw an opportunity to speak into the lives of men who needed to hear the liberating good news of the gospel of Jesus Christ, and I needed money, so it was a good fit.

When I started working my sons kidded me that it was the first time I worked a real job for thirty years. There was some truth to that. In what is considered full-time ministry I enjoyed considerable flexibility which would be lost in 9–5 employment. An additional concern was that after thirty years in ministry, with four earned degrees and two French language diplomas, I had no idea what kind of work I could find. I discovered that is not an uncommon scenario for men with ministry training. My advice for younger men today would be to gain some skills and experience in another area. Urban church planting will often require that you become bi-vocational. So I went to prison, or as you will see, back to prison. For almost three years from early 2011 to late 2013 I had the opportunity to work as an addiction therapist in the Philadelphia Prison System. Therapy was one area considered "related" to the theological training and degrees I had accumulated. Growing up, my family had a close relationship to the prison. My father had been a correctional officer for over twenty years at Holmesburg Prison and the Detention Center. One of my aunts was a correctional officer at the House of Correction which in the 70s was divided in sections to house both men and women. On top of that, my former brother-in-law was Prison Commissioner in the late 90s until around 2006. None of that made me an expert in criminal justice although in time I became a Certified Criminal Justice Professional. Yet my time in prison gave me a perspective I want to share.

One of the prisons I worked in was where I had been incarcerated briefly in the early 70s when arrested and charged with burglary, receiving stolen goods, and whatever was added to the list. At the time I was seventeen years old and normally would've been taken to the local district police station. However, my dad had made many trips to pick me up at the 25th District police station, then at Front & Westmoreland Sts., and warned me that he was not coming anymore. That meant I had a good chance of going to the dreaded Youth Study Center (which always seemed like an odd name for a juvenile detention facility). The police took me first to the district for booking and questioning. I had what seemed like a brilliant idea at the time, at least to my teenage brain. I lied about my age and gave a false birthdate. I suppose that in pre-computer times it wasn't that easy to crosscheck dates. Or maybe they simply believed me. I mean, really, who lies about their age in order to risk more trouble? With a stroke of a pen I was born a year earlier, 1953 instead of 1954, which made me eighteen years old. As such, my parents would not be called. I would go to the Roundhouse at 8th & Race Sts. and be released on my own recognizance, or so I thought. Instead of being released, I was given $1000 bail which meant coming up with $100. I had no money and no friends who would come up with that sum of money. I was placed in a van with other prisoners and taken to State Road where the prisons are lined up. There was one hitch. At that time, before the construction of the Curran-Fromhold Correctional Facility (CFCF), incoming prisoners were processed at the Detention Center (DC) where my dad worked. I knew I would not be allowed to be in the same jail with my dad. As we were shuffling out of the police van I whispered to one of the van drivers, "My dad works here." The guard separated me from the other inmates, made a phone call, placed me back in the van by myself, and drove me to the House of Corrections (HOC). Although my Aunt Mary worked there at the time, she was on the women's side, and I could be incarcerated on the men's side. My aunt came to see me accompanied by a captain when her shift started. She told me she would call my mom and if my mom wanted me home, my aunt would put up the money to bail me out. You might guess that my mom wanted me released. My aunt paid my bail with a stern warning to show up for court or else.

My first days back in prison working rather than imprisoned were a wonderful reminder of how God changed my life. I knew that it was only by God's grace that I wasn't incarcerated or dead. After receiving my security clearance, I plunged into my work with eagerness and soon became known as a no-nonsense counselor who was fair and firm. Having grown up in Philly I made easy connections with most of the men I worked with. They knew where I was from. They knew without the details that I had some drug and criminal-related background. I never tried to pretend that I was a tough guy, back then or now. Whenever possible I pointed men to Jesus Christ as the one who could change not only their lives but their eternal destiny. There was no coercion to believe in God or embrace religion or a particular denomination. Much of the conversation came up naturally. Men were curious and surprised, especially once they heard my background, about why I would work in a prison. In time I became close to some of the men who were there for longer periods and even now stay in touch with some who were sentenced to terms in state prison. I ran several groups in prison. Many of these were traditional group sessions—educational groups on drugs, criminal thinking and behavior, Twelve Step meetings, etc. In addition, I was permitted to hold weekly Bible studies. It was made clear to men that Bible study was not required, and the men had to sign a consent form to show they were there voluntarily. There was so much interest in Bible study that I had to limit the number of attendees to those I felt were interested in more than just getting off the block for a couple hours a week.

When I first started working at the prison, all the men we worked with were in one prison on one block. At the time we had three counselors for about one hundred men, a suite of offices and a group room. These men were housed at the Philadelphia Industrial Correctional Center (PICC) which was a newer facility with restricted movement, that is, the units were self-contained. Inmates did not go to a common dining hall but had meals brought to them, and medication distribution and counseling took place with as little movement as possible. PICC was considered maximum security which was the reason for stricter security measures. Each morning when I entered the prison, I went through a metal detector and underwent a cursory pat down by male or female guards. I carried a special card which gave security clearance to all the prisons on State Road. This card was obtained after a rigorous background check and two days of security training at

Holmesburg Prison, now used mostly for administrative functions. Once screened at the security desk I entered a series of doors, about six or seven, which were operated electronically by someone in the "bubble." You would push a button to signal your presence. Sometimes either the buttons didn't work or the guards in the bubble weren't paying attention. You waited until you were buzzed through the door, then the next door, then . . . well you get the picture. I never had any interest in working as a prison guard but if I did I would not want to work in the bubble. It's hard to imagine a more mind-numbing job but it was a job and I suppose some people coveted being locked in the bubble pushing buttons all day in between reading the newspaper and whatever else went on in there.

There was always some stress in getting into and out of the prison even though you knew you were getting out at the end of the day. There is something about impatiently waiting for someone to push a button, your powerlessness to move without their consent, the doors clanging behind you, and crossing inmates in the hallway. We were supposed to carry a body alarm and occasionally they would ask to see it upon entering the prison. For a long time, I carried one without batteries. No one ever checked for that and nobody wanted you to pull out the pin for an ear-piercing test. I never felt threatened in the prison and any incidents I had were minor verbal ones. Which was a good thing since the response to alarms was slow or none. In my office there was a red button that when pushed set off the alarms in the hallway and in the unit bubble. On two occasions the button was pushed and the alarm set off accidentally by inmates who leaned back on a chair. No one came to my office. I would go to the bubble and tell them it was accidentally set off. Eventually they would send someone with a key to turn it off, once they found the right key. Early on I was not impressed with the overall competence of the prison system.

My time back in the prison system ended when I left to work in a clinic as a therapist then moved on to become a clinical supervisor. One thought that comes to my mind often is that in prison we had Bible studies where I freely and openly spoke of salvation in Christ. There is freedom to preach the gospel once people are incarcerated. Yet in our schools the Bible has been banned. Something wrong there. But that is the system. Also, readers should know that I was walked out of the prison on my last day by two officers, a captain and a major, asked to surrender my credentials, and subsequently stripped of my security clearance as part of retaliation for doing my job. Twice I had to report officers. One was a guard who let two prisoners in a cell to beat and rob another inmate. It was on camera. When I reported it, an officer let me see the video which was clear as day. The offending guard was moved off that block and transferred to another. Nothing more. Another was a lieutenant who I reported for misconduct who then sought revenge. When I reported her, both the prison warden and his assistant came to see me and let me know they "spoke" with the lieutenant. Two guards on my block warned me that she had it in for me. She did and she had her pound of flesh. There was no investigation of which I was a part and in my requests for clarification I was rebuffed and simply told that my security clearance would never be restored. I discovered how insular the prison system was and that there was a loyalty code between prison workers that was more important than the truth. Doing the right thing will not always bring good consequences. I was also told I would never be allowed back in the prisons where I worked which has become a joke with me wondering what happens if I'm ever arrested in Philadelphia. Where will they take me?

Chapter 6

Two Fundamental Questions

OVER THE YEARS I have had the opportunity to meet young men preparing to plant urban churches. Many of their primary supporting and sending churches have great ministries, mostly in suburban or rural areas. In some places, there were certain emphases in dress standards, meeting times, with doctrinal statements exhibiting great precision, and traditional music. An emphasis on separation issues and cultural taboos often prevented church members from having meaningful relationships with people outside the church. These are observations gathered in discussions and not meant as criticisms. As a matter of fact, these churches often have effective ministries with Christians although they see few non-Christians coming to Christ. The churches have been built and have grown primarily by adding Christians who left cities or with Christians from other churches who move into the area. The churches have established niche ministries ministering to Christians. In other words, these churches have their place in the world and God uses them although many are stuck in expressions of cultural Christianity which rarely engage non-Christians.

Prospective urban church planters often find themselves in a dilemma. The churches they envision planting share the core theological convictions of their mother churches yet there are traditional practices, more cultural than biblical, which they feel need to be shed in a new church plant. The church planters ask themselves: Do I retain the status quo and model the new church after the mother church and wait to introduce change in a few years when the ministry is independent and self-sustainable? Or do I transparently express my intentions to the mother church and risk withdrawal of support and burned bridges?

Planting new churches is a daunting task that like matrimony must not be entered lightly. When people ask me how to plant a church, what steps need to be taken, I try to explain that church planting is more of an art than a science and with many surprises. You make lots of plans, but the unfolding of God's purposes takes place stroke by stroke. There must not only be a personal conviction that God has called you to church planting but affirmation from others that you are so called.

Church planting involves numerous details such as strategy, demographic studies, fundraising, location, and gathering a leadership and launch team. The reality soon sets in that you are not adequate for the task. It is God's work and without him you labor in vain. However, before launching into this most noble and challenging of endeavors there are two questions you need to ask and answer. Whom are you trying to please? Whom do you want to reach? How church planters answer these questions will help determine their direction in church planting. This is how I answer church planters.

Whom are you trying to please? The first question should receive an evident response. You want to please God, not man. However, you will be tempted to look over your shoulder to see what others think of what you are doing. You might be surprised at how many people think that new churches should dance to the same tune as churches which have existed for decades with their well-established traditions. The traditions are not necessarily wrong but may be unnecessary barriers in planting an urban church among those unacquainted with those traditions. Doing ministry differently than it has been done by your peers and potential supporting churches often invites intense scrutiny and criticism.

Certainly, you should avoid offending Christians by intentionally creating controversy or championing causes that are divisive. You want to transparently say that this is who you are, this is how you live, and this is what you understand that God wants you to do. Yet you want to be discreet and not accentuate those areas where you might not be following traditions and opinions held firmly by some. In other words, you should not poke your fingers in the eyes of Christians and churches who see and who practice some things differently than you do. You want to be biblical, not edgy but with an edge, and always pushing further into your understanding of the outworking of God's purposes in the church and in the world.

Whom do you want to reach? The second question should likewise elicit an obvious response. You want to reach people without Christ. However, you might be tempted to take stock of the kind of Christians who find their way to your door and cater to their preferences and expectations. Please don't misunderstand me. You want to meet Christians where they are and would be delighted if God led them to journey with you. In fact, you should ask God to create a launch team of Christians to partner with you in church planting. But you ask them to come with humility and with a teachable spirit. You might need to ask them to be open to different forms of worship, a different leadership style, a different philosophy of ministry, and a different way of living out practical Christianity. You must not be bent on upsetting Christians or seeking to undermine what they believe about the church and the Christian life. You must have complete confidence in the authority of Scripture and the power of the Spirit to transform lives. You want to follow God's Word, not human agendas, not even your own.

New churches are planted to make Christ known to those who do not know him or do not know Christ as presented in the Bible. These people may have heard of him. They may be acquainted with those who profess to know him. Yet they do not yet have a saving and loving relationship with him and the Father. Therefore, as much as lies within you as a Christian and as a church, you do not want to erect unbiblical and unnecessary barriers which prevent others from a hearing of the good news and a redemptive encounter with Christ. Never be fearful that some may be offended by the truth of the gospel but be careful that the offense is related to truth and not to how you articulate it or live it out. At the same time, do not chase relevancy for you will soon be irrelevant.

A note of caution: you do not need to be uber cool and shock people with your dress, your appearance, your wisps of facial hair, your gold chains, your cap turned backward, your ripped jeans. Do not do things in ways to draw unnecessary attention to yourself. The church of Jesus Christ does not need more superstars or slobs in the pulpit. Leave your cool jeans at home, especially if they are skinny jeans. Spend little time on getting your pompadour just right. Being bald does have its benefits. You do not need to be known as the fun church where people come to be entertained with the band and background smoke with groovy images on the screen. You may build a large something that way, but it will not be a faithful church.

In answering these two questions church planters should not deliberately irritate supporting churches or needlessly alienate Christians by emphasizing differences in a way that is divisive. Neither should church planters be expected to adhere to extrabiblical, albeit longstanding traditions which would be impositions on a new church and deform its identity. There should be mutual respect and humility between church planters and their sending churches. Church planters should not have any illusions about being able to perfectly balance the response to these two questions. They must simply desire to plant God's church, a grace-filled, gospel-centered church, and journey together with those whom God calls alongside them to accomplish his purposes in urban America.

Chapter 7

Dangers of Cultural Accommodation

Cultural accommodation is a genuine danger in planting churches. However, the real problem is the one-sided perspective that many have of accommodation. The accommodation is sometimes seen rightly, but narrowly, in relation only to the world. Frequently forgotten is cultural accommodation toward Christians. This is generally well-meaning but misguided. There are Christians who have a truncated view of the Christian life and seek to impose discipleship and the Christian life as they have known and experienced it as normative for all believers. Thus, there are twin dangers of cultural accommodation: 1) Accommodating or catering to the unchurched in designing worship from a seeker-driven mentality; 2) Accommodating or catering to the churched who come to the new church plant with their preferences paraded mistakenly for biblical convictions.

In the previous chapter I mentioned two questions to ask in church planting: "Whom are you trying to please?" and "Whom do you want to reach?" The point was that in pleasing God and reaching the lost you might upset many believers who probably shouldn't care so much about what you do in your church. As an aside, I think churches with longstanding traditions should tread carefully and lay a clear biblical foundation for needed biblical change. If that foundation isn't laid or can't be laid, then whether and what change should be pursued has to be re-examined. Without needed renewal some churches might die but it won't do to simply chase the latest fad. In church planting it's less a question of change than it is of determining the right course from the beginning. There is not the same importance accorded to peripheral issues as there is in churches with established practice.

Most unbelievers do not care what Bible version your church plant uses, what preferences leadership might hold concerning dress standards, or what musical philosophy you hold, at least not at the outset. The greater problem in planting a new church is what Christians expect to find in the new church—their favorite Bible version, their opinions on what music God listens to, an American flag on the platform, and their lists of do's and don'ts deemed emblems of true spirituality which in reality is religious moralism.

Concerning the first danger mentioned above of accommodating the unchurched, there is biblical warrant for having worship done in such a way that unbelievers come under conviction and "worship God and declare that God is really among you" (1 Cor 14:25). That does not mean that you entertain them in a show atmosphere or dilute the gospel to make it more palatable with "plausible words of wisdom" (1 Cor 2:4). It does mean that you need to engage them with the truth in a comprehensible way. If we use incomprehensible words in our witness to unbelievers with the lame reasoning that the Holy Spirit will enlighten them, we abdicate our responsibility to "make it clear, which is how [we] ought to speak" (Col 4:4). Further, "we have to wrestle with the reasons why people reject the gospel, and in particular give due weight to the cultural factors. Some people reject the gospel not because they perceive it to be false, but because they perceive it to be alien."[1] We cannot do the Spirit's work of bringing conviction. We can do the "work of an evangelist" and speak simply and clearly the words of life. In other words, let the gospel offend but don't excuse your personal offensiveness in saying you're only preaching the Bible. Surely the natural man doesn't receive the things of the

1. Stott, "World Evangelization," 24.

Spirit of God (1 Cor 2:14). That's no reason for a lack of courtesy, attentiveness, humility, and civility in speaking the light into darkness. That's no excuse for adding your own opinions to the demands of Christ.

Concerning the second danger mentioned above of accommodating the churched, there is biblical warrant for believers to be like-minded (Phil 2:2; 1 Pet 3:8). It is interesting to me that these texts which enjoin like-mindedness among believers also call respectively for "having the same love" and "brotherly love." How rarely we find these today in issue-driven churches! These virtues do not entail unanimity in all that we believe to be important for the Christian life. Whether we admit it or not we are all influenced by our backgrounds, education, discipleship environments and mentors, which cause us to emphasize some issues out of proportion to their scriptural importance or biblical clarity. Of course, there are some who are right on all issues, who claim the final word on disputed matters and continue to pass judgment on other believers notwithstanding the apostolic prohibition (Rom 14:13).

Part of my observation in an earlier chapter mentioned dress, music, and Bible versions. Their mention was not meant as a criticism of those who choose differently in those areas. Although I have no problem with those who would make different choices in these areas, I resist vigorously any attempt to have someone speak for me in a once-for-all fashion as if they have the one right position. And tragically these issues have become fodder for endless disputations particularly by those who, whether from naïve realism or under the spell of influential gurus, have exalted their preferences to a level of scriptural certainty. Those who disagree are disobedient to Scripture, preach another gospel, or are possibly apostates.

So, in planting a new church this is what by God's grace we as leaders should do when facing the dangers of accommodating culture, whether it be contemporary culture or preferential, Christianized culture which vaunts itself as the only true expression and representation of biblical Christianity. Concerning the unchurched, we boldly and uncompromisingly preach the gospel of salvation by grace in Christ alone. Yet, "we need to be reminded that this gospel is not simply an evangelism plan; it is a message of how the good news of God's provisions affects our whole lives every day."[2] With that in mind, we do not require that new believers submit to a list of regulations—"Do not handle, do not taste, do not touch" (Col 2:21)—to achieve spiritual maturity. We seek to be a welcoming church, but we will not affirm all the choices people make. We are confident in the power of the Word and Spirit to bring authentic transformation rather than superficial conformity in the lives of God's people. We want God to produce followers of Christ not imitators of men.

Concerning the churched, we welcome them to journey with us in discovering more about grace. Come, we say, let us worship the Lord in the beauty of holiness. Come with your KJV, ESV, NASB or NIV but if you need to prove to everyone that you have determined which translation is best for everyone else then you might be ill at ease among us with our tainted translations. Come with your suits and ties, wing-tipped shoes, skirts, slacks or Dockers, jeans, pullovers, and sandals. But if you have an impulse to establish the proper dress code or beard and hair lengths so worship is acceptable to God then you won't be happy with the way we look. Come with your preferences for classical hymns, gospel choruses, contemporary praise songs, ethnic flavors, and we will incorporate from these that which we believe is fitting to honor the majesty and glory of our God and Savior. Say "Amen," clap your hands, lift your hands or remain silent and meditative. But if you must always agree with musical choices and modes of expression and have an agenda to correct faulty worship then it might be best to start your own church. Come with your convictions and precisions of the timing and interpretation of end-time events. Leave your prophetic charts at home. Let us look together for the coming of Christ and his eternal kingdom without being obsessed with speculative details. Come with your questions and opinions on Calvinism and Arminianism but leave a dogmatic, argumentative, crusading spirit at the door. We believe

---

2. Chapell, *Christ-Centered Worship*, 100.

in sovereign grace and amazing grace. We do not magnify one without the other. We do not fully comprehend either or claim a divine perspective. We preach "whosoever will may come" and "whosoever will not" does not come.

In our attempt to be faithful followers of Jesus Christ, we seek neither accommodation to the world nor accommodation to cultural expressions of Christianity. We embrace truth yet have no illusion that we and we alone have grasped it fully. We submit to that truth to shape the church which Christ builds.

Chapter 8

Some Nuts and Bolts

IN A PREVIOUS CHAPTER we looked at some of the challenges in planting urban churches. That chapter dealt primarily with the temptation to accommodate culture—traditional Christian cultural expressions or contemporary culture. There are significant challenges in planting churches anywhere. However, there are special challenges in planting urban churches. It is unquestionable that the majority of middle-class evangelical Christians live in the suburbs and that certain regions sprout new churches like mushrooms thanks to a large Christian population and multiple churches from which to draw.

In planting a suburban church in many areas of North America there is a greater likelihood of finding a core group of believers to help start a new church along with adequate resources. As a matter of fact, one of the best methods of starting a new church is with a mother church encouraging members to help with the new church plant, whether temporarily on loan from the mother church or in it for the long haul. When we moved to Philadelphia in 2009 we were blessed with several families and individuals who lived in the suburbs and served with us in the city. Ideally we would have liked to see them make the decision to move into the city in order to be truly incarnational in their witness. However, it is not our job to make that call for people although we do encourage Christians to consider if God might have them make what for many would be a great sacrifice in relocating to the city. We find that single adults and younger couples are more open to this challenge and see their choice as response to a calling which involves sacrifice for the gospel and the kingdom of Christ rather than simply making career choices which lead to upward mobility. We also find that once couples start having children many move from the city for different reasons but often poor school choices is among them. In our experience suburban Christians who assist in the formative months or years of an urban church plant eventually return to their suburban church. And that's okay.

I have heard Christians tell me that they could not live in a big city or they do not want to raise children in a city where the "reality of inner-city life is absorbed largely on the streets."[1] I understand that and realize that city life is not for everyone and is not God's calling for their lives and ministry. People who are willing to invest in the city need to know that city life presents unique challenges. A quick glance at the news makes it clear that there are no safe, crime-free, drug-free places in our country. And wherever we are, the greatest safety is in our Lord's care wherever we might live. What is different in many cities is the concentration of crime, drug addiction, homelessness, ex-cons, boarding houses, and warehouses for people suffering from mental health problems. These problems are in your face every day. They are in your church to some degree. I shouldn't have been surprised at how many people attending services at our church have spent time in prison. At times we have had a higher percentage of ex-cons and former addicts attending than in any church I've ever been a part of. Also, at times more people with PhDs. Living in the city requires a pioneer spirit and a willingness to be confronted daily with the grittier side of life.

On the practical side, finding a meeting place often seems like an impossible quest. Many urban churches will never find property on which to build a church-style building and may remain renters

1. Anderson, *Code of the Street*, 69.

for many years. Limited resources, high unemployment, and skyrocketing real estate costs present formidable obstacles. Some of the best real estate is occupied by mainline churches that no longer preach the gospel if they ever did. Other church buildings have been turned into condominiums. Areas where real estate is available and affordable are often places which are the most troubled. Many church planters will need to be bi-vocational since more people attending does not necessarily translate into more giving in the offering. Hence the encouragement to have marketable skills.

Pockets of poverty can be found almost anywhere but there is a greater concentration of poverty in urban areas accompanied by quality of life issues. And some urban areas are more impoverished than others. Philadelphia has the distinction of being the poorest of the ten largest cities in the US with the highest percentage of people living in poverty and double the poverty rate of the rest of the state (Philly News September 13, 2017). Depending on the community in which you plant you may have a greater number of people on welfare and unemployed or unemployable. You will be called upon to give not only of yourself but of your material goods. Growth in numbers attending may not result in more giving to the ministry of the church. Growth may be costlier as the church addresses deep physical and material needs. Of course not all urban churches are alike and one's experiences will not exactly mirror the experiences of others. Just as there are pockets of poverty in urban areas there are pockets of wealth and many neighborhoods have undergone gentrification to the point that housing costs prohibit all but the well-heeled to purchase a home.

Church planters must come to grips with the reality that there is no guarantee of success in church planting if by success you think of having a large, self-supporting church with its own facilities. God measures success differently and considers faithfulness the measure of ministry. I have witnessed the birth of many churches which have folded after a year or two for various reasons—lack of finances, discouragement, and family problems to name a few. It is important to go into church planting with confidence in God and not depend on your own abilities, strategy, models, or marketing. All of these have a place but dependence on them may lead to reliance on what you are doing and thinking that you can plant a church because you have the training, finances, and previous ministry experience.

Church planters will need to raise support, build a ministry team, gather a core group, find a place to live, find a place to meet, and determine when to start services. Before any of those details are worked out church planters should have thought through and prayed through issues relating to philosophy of ministry. Are you going to target a certain group in following a homogeneous model or simply preach the gospel and pray that God would bring together people which reflect the community? In Philadelphia we are in a diverse community. Hence we committed to planting a multi-ethnic church. Being committed to this doesn't mean it will happen as we would like. However, we want people to know that they are welcome among us regardless of ethnicity, age, educational level, or economic status. We do not want to cater to any one demographic component of our community. In saying that, keep in mind that there is nothing wrong with planting a homogeneous church if that represents your demographics.

Church planters also need to determine whether the church will be issue-centered or Christ-centered. Issue-centered churches will be concerned about enforcing high standards, taking the right position on schools, music, versions, proper Sunday dress, and eschewing Christian fellowship with other Bible-believing churches that differ on minor doctrinal or denominational questions. Christ-centered, gospel-driven churches will boldly preach Christ and expect Spirit-produced transformation which results in obedience to the Word and not to human dictates.

Let me mention an area of possible difference between church planters and pastors. Pastors who are called to a church have many questions already answered for them by what has been established as the norm over time. As one pastor friend says, a pastor may need to stop watering certain plants and let them die. That's good advice if accepting a call to an established ministry. To introduce radical and/or unnecessary change may be disruptive and appear disrespectful of the previous pastor. Even if some of the traditions are more 1950s than first century, great care must be exercised in introducing change and the change must be directed by the Word of God not by personal whims, fancies, or latest church growth marketing. Given the nature of their ministries, different perspectives between church planters and established pastors are not surprising. Yet, how those differences affect the ability to partner remains crucial. There is the possibility of great misunderstanding between the new church plant and sending churches or potential supporting churches. We have experienced this firsthand. We have two churches who provide support on a regular basis—Sonship Ministries in Brooklyn, which tithes on its offerings each month to our church, and Fellowship Bible Church, an established church in northeast Philadelphia. The rest of our support over the years has come from individuals. All our elders are either retired or bi-vocational except for the lead pastor. You might also find that many churches will be more generous toward missionaries "over there," even if engaged in ministry that does not lead to planting churches, than "here" at home. Get used to encountering the mentality that missionaries are people who leave their country to do something somewhere else.

Before returning to Philadelphia to plant a new church I had discussions with several pastor friends. Although they appreciated what we were doing and were personally supportive, they felt their church could not partner with us. For some it was a constitutional matter (which they often inherited) that stipulated agreement to the nth degree. For others it was the sensitivities of church members who would react to a church not using the same translation, the same music, the same polity, and the same name. I understood that and did not travel church-to-church to raise support. I took a job instead and presently work several days a week as a certified addiction therapist. In short, I am not surprised that some pastors disagreed with what we were doing. Theirs is a different calling, with different gifts, and different perspectives. Although I have been asked, I have never accepted a call as senior pastor. That does not mean I never would. Yet, I am not sure that I am ready at my age (64 at the time of writing) or have what it takes to pastor a church long-term and to have inherited buildings, prime location, place of influence, and financial stability (and I realize that not all pastors inherit that). I am not being critical of that scenario. It may be that I am not gifted in that way. That is God's calling and equipping upon the lives of these men. I admire pastors who take a church and stay for decades. My ministry has been broader than most but perhaps not as deep as those who labor in one place for many years. Yet I rejoice that God has given me the privilege of planting churches in Philadelphia, France, and Romania, and of providing pastoral training in other nations as well.

Those who have never actively planted a new church, who have never met in their living room, who have never had only their family and wondering who else might show up, and who have never worked bi-vocationally to support their family, will not have the same questions and/or answers as church planters. That is to be expected. It is not that pastors could not plant a church. Many of them are gifted in leadership and preaching where they could plant a church if that was what God called them to do. I am not arguing for one being better than the other. But it is different and some of those differences cannot be understood until you've walked in the church planter's shoes.

Several times I have alluded to the importance of a husband and wife both seeing their calling for the city. This is one area that cannot be overemphasized. My brother John and I both have wives from the Midwest who did not grow up in a large city and perhaps preferred suburban life at one point. Yet in their commitment to the Lord and to us they have not only adapted but in many ways have thrived in the city, although I cannot be sure it is their preference. John and I have personally known several couples who were committed to urban church planting and did not last long in the city. There was a dream. There was excitement. There was perhaps a romantic and unrealistic view of urban ministry. There was naivete. But there was not unity. John reminded me of one young man who shared with him his passion for urban church planting with enthusiasm. John asked what his wife thought and if she had ever lived in a city. The young man said she was a little reluctant but would adjust. They came and left after a few years because of her inability to adjust. We have seen similar scenarios repeat themselves over and over. Of course, there is urban and there is inner city. There are some oases in the city that feel almost suburban. Yet if someone has never studied, lived, or worked in the city with its congestion, noise, barking dogs, crime, and in some places its filthy streets, the gap to bridge is too wide.

My wife and I live in West Philly, notorious for its crime rates. Our neighborhood, however, with its tree-lined streets has benefited from gentrification. Apart from the occasional burglary attempt, cars broken into, assault or armed robbery, there is relative calm. It is not my neighbors committing these crimes. Three of my neighbors are university professors or researchers with PhDs. Three blocks away it is a different world and that world bleeds into ours. When we walk at night after dinner, we plan our route according to the time of day. If it is dark, we go in a direction that is "safer." If it is light, we feel we can go in another direction toward a park that is okay during the day. My wife rarely goes out by herself at night. I have a carry permit and hope I am never in a situation to have to defend myself. I am not that concerned about myself. I worked in the prison system for several years. I understand some of the criminal mentality. Criminals usually look for the easy target. Looking at me they might (or might not) pass me up for someone who appears less able to resist, or as we see often, people oblivious to their surroundings talking on their cellphone or listening to music. We call that "apple pickin'" when someone runs by and grabs your phone or earbuds. I want to yell at people, "Get your face out of your phone!" And if you have a backpack that is icing on the cake. Laptops are especially prized. In the city you need awareness of your surroundings and some bravado, even if faked. If you grew up in Philly you can do the Philly stroll and look like no one should mess with you. All that to say simply that it may be too much to expect someone to adapt who has never known city life. Be sure of your calling and of your ability to adapt to city life. Perhaps even do an internship before you take the leap. For some, city life is what they've known and they navigate with relative ease. For others, city life is an acquired taste that takes some major adjustments. And then there are those who cannot adapt and will function better in a different environment. As Socrates and others purportedly said, "Know thyself!" I would add, "Know thy wife and listen to her!"

Chapter 9

Why Some Church Planters Never Plant Churches

I HAVE OFTEN ASKED church planters the following questions: How has God prepared you in your training and experience for this task? What evidence do you have in your ministry to date that demonstrates the likelihood of effectiveness in church planting? What strategy do you have for planting a contextualized church? How much have you studied the history and culture of your place of calling? After a few uncomfortable moments and a glazed-over stare I am assured of God's call upon them and that they are going by faith but receive no answers to the questions. A semi-mystical call seems to answer all. Many of these church planters will never plant a church and it's not always their fault. Churches in partnership must become more intentional in the selection process and in filling in the gaps in church planters' preparation. They cannot be prepared for all they will face. But they can be better prepared and be assured that by God's grace they have done all they can to be equipped for the Master's service and ready to engage in effective ministry for the glory of God.

Over the years, as I have travelled and taught and planted churches, I have reflected on the dearth of church planting that takes place in many places where church planters labor for years.

True, there are places where there is a greater openness to the gospel and God has prepared the soil. Yet in many places there is often little fruit to show for the labor. When prospective church planters are sent from churches which do not plant churches where they are, it comes as no surprise that few churches are being planted in other places. Many church planters have been discipled in a maintenance ministry rather than in a multiplication ministry. The only church life they have experienced has been in a church that focused on member care and which had never been involved in planting churches. While these same churches provide support for missionaries who plant churches "over there," they neglect to plant churches "over here" in their own North American context.

We have heard for several years that North America is one of the great unreached mission fields. Yet many churches continue their solitary existence with some thought but little action toward planting another church in their town, their state, or their country, and commit few resources to accomplish what remains one of the great omissions in many Bible-believing churches. The question must be asked as to why most established churches never plant other churches and after decades of existence cannot point to another church they have planted. One of the problems faced by many churches is that they lack networks for partnership in church planting. There are denominational and associational movements with unquestionable evangelical commitments that are active in planting churches. They have something to teach us. Many churches simply lack the resources to plant churches on their own while other churches with resources may refuse to partner with church planters unless the new church looks like the supporting church. Will they emphasize the right version, have the right polity, use the right name, practice the right standards, and employ the right music? There must be criteria for supporting church planters. Yet overly stringent demands may lead to supporting church planters who plant only ineffective church clones.

Many churches have relegated missions to one of the programs of the church, competing for resources with member-care ministries that provide more visual bang or immediate benefits.

Why Some Church Planters Never Plant Churches

This is a theological problem and has been echoed by others who hold that "in the ecclesiocentric approach of Christendom, mission became only one of the programs of the church. . . . But it has taken us decades to realize that mission is not just a program of the church. It defines the church as God's sent people."[1] Certainly there are churches that are missionary or mission-minded and will designate a small percentage of their income to support missionary activities in what is often called "foreign" missions. However, recent studies have shown that "the money given by the people in the pews . . . is largely spent on the people in the pews. Only about 3 percent of money donated to churches and ministries went to aiding or ministering to non-Christians."[2] Now some might argue that this is only one measurement of a church's priorities. Perhaps, but it cannot be ignored. Think about this for a moment. Does mission or missional really define your church? Ask yourself as a pastor or as a member of a church what percentage of what comes into your church goes out for ministry that does not immediately benefit your congregation. Does that lead to an uncomfortable stroke of conviction? We build institutions, establish programs, and create numerous para-church ministries. For what purpose? Are we concerned primarily with ministry for the benefit and comfort of believers? Certainly the church must be concerned with the edification and education of its church members. But when this leads to neglect in multiplying reproductive churches it is time to reorient our focus.

Planting a new church usually takes far longer than anyone imagined, and it is not getting easier to plant churches in our present cultural climate. I understand the enormous challenges, the investment and sacrifice needed to launch a church plant. I recounted earlier how in 1982 my wife and I were sent to plant a church in Philadelphia, my hometown. I was fresh out of seminary and we moved back into the city. God gave us a small core of people, my wife worked full-time for a few months, and our sending church gave us a small weekly paycheck. I taught Sunday

---

1. Guder, *Missional Church*, 6.
2. "Scrooge Lives," *Christianity Today Online*, December 5, 2008.

School, led the singing (I know that's scary), preached the morning service, the evening service, and the Wednesday night service. I did my best which meant I often scrambled to study and now know that no one should be expected to preach and teach well that many times a week. My wife played the piano, worked in the nursery, taught children, and did ladies' Bible studies. We knocked on doors and received new move-in contacts from Welcome Wagon. Within one year we were self-supporting, and my wife was able to quit her job. We rented four locations in as many years before God allowed us to purchase a church building replete with beautiful stained-glass windows and a huge pipe organ. Christ built his church and allowed us to be co-laborers with Him.

Yet times have changed. In some ways the challenges are more daunting in church planting than in the past. On one hand, more and more churches are planted by teams, as it should be when possible. More time is taken to prepare for a church launch in order to constitute a committed core of people that will enhance the sustainability of the ministry. More attention is given to demographic studies in order to better understand the target groups. On the other hand, door-to-door evangelism can no longer be done in many areas. Rental costs have skyrocketed. Team ministry requires more resources to send and sustain a team in place. There are higher expectations by attendees and prospective members in the area of facilities and technology. Christianity has moved more from the mainstream to the margins of society, particularly in urban areas which were largely forsaken by evangelical churches during white flight to the suburbs. Happily, there is a refreshing call today for Christians to return to the cities from the safety and sameness of their utopian suburbs, to reject monocultural homogeneity in order to embrace divinely-ordered diversity, to reclaim ground that has been lost to triumphant secularism, and to engage the culture of ideas in urban centers of education and the arts. All this in order to preach Christ in the densely populated, multi-cultural arenas of spiritual warfare and to live as Christians in community in neighborhoods that have been broken by sin and are filled with despair.

Churches that will not partner with other churches, that will not invest significantly in supporting church planting teams, and that continue to concentrate on themselves in an exclusionary way will not plant many churches. They will however miss out on many of God's blessings and fail to accomplish numerous purposes for which God planted their churches in the first place. How refreshing and spiritually delightful it would be to see in our time more churches at the forefront of church planting and for God's glory!

Chapter 10

Church and Kingdom in the City

I WANT TO CLOSE with one major theological and practical issue you will face in the city which relates to the church and kingdom dynamic and the mission of the church. As N. T. Wright observes, the phrase "kingdom of God has been a flag of convenience under which all sorts of ships have sailed."[1] These ships are social, political, nationalistic, and theological. Their corresponding agendas often have little to do with the arrival of the kingdom of God announced by Jesus.

The opening of the gospel of Mark proclaims the "beginning of the gospel of Jesus Christ." Jesus arrives on the scene, "preaching the gospel of God" (1:14). He announces that "the time is fulfilled; the kingdom of God is near. Repent and believe in the gospel" (v. 15). The phrase "is near" can be understood as referring to something still to happen. However, as France comments, "If Jesus is understood to have proclaimed as 'near' something which had still not arrived even at the time when Mark wrote his gospel (let alone 2,000 years later), this is hardly less of an embarrassment than if he had claimed that 'it' was already present."[2]

---

1. Wright, *Surprised by Hope*, 203.
2. France, *Mark*, 92.

Church and Kingdom in the City

There are passages which indicate a present kingdom aspect (Luke 17:21) and others which point to a future aspect (Matt 25:34; Luke 21:17, 31). Multiple texts demonstrate that the gospel of the kingdom was the message of Jesus and the apostles (Luke 4:43; 9:1, 2). Jesus "instructed the seventy to proclaim, 'The kingdom of God has come near to you'" (Luke 10:1, 9). In Acts we find Philip who "preached good news about the kingdom of God and the name of Jesus Christ . . . ." (Acts 8:12). The Apostle Paul in Ephesus "entered the synagogue and for three months spoke boldly, reasoning and persuading them about the kingdom of God" (Acts 19:8). Near the end of his ministry, Paul "expounded to them, testifying to the kingdom of God." (Acts 28:23).

Any initiation of a present aspect of the kingdom must be distinguished from the consummation of the future kingdom. According to Ladd, "the Kingdom of God involves two great moments: fulfillment within history, and consummation at the end of history."[3] The reality of future completion does not rule out present kingdom realties and there is no area of human life or culture which is not subject to Jesus' authority, where the gospel does not speak with power. While there is certainly a greater fullness and understanding of the gospel following the death, burial, and resurrection of Jesus Christ, is there any valid reason, apart from the impositions of a theological system, to deny that there is both a present aspect of reign of God among his people and an eschatological consummation?

Many churches ministering in urban areas see social concerns rooted in spiritual problems, problems to which the gospel speaks through the message of salvation bringing transformation, granting eternal life and offering new life in Christ here and now. In short, the gospel of the kingdom, the good news of God's reign already inaugurated in the first coming of Christ, authenticated by his earthly ministry in confronting and defeating the forces of evil, visibly and divinely demonstrated in the death, burial, resurrection, and session of Christ at the right hand of the Father, and consummated at his return in glory—this is the gospel we preach!

3. Ladd, *Presence of the Future*, 118.

It is not only a gospel for the hereafter, which would be enough if that was God's intention; it is also a gospel for life here and now. It is not all about not being "left behind" or getting to heaven. "For Jesus, God's kingdom was fundamentally God's reign over the lives of men and women."[4]

One reason for renewed interest in this subject is that the gospel of the kingdom has been expanded and associated with understandings of the kingdom and mission of the church which go beyond a traditional and biblical focus on evangelism and discipleship. Let me be clear. There is no kingdom ministry without the gospel. In preaching the gospel, we believe that the gospel brings new creation to individuals and bears firstfruits of the eschatological new creation through the authority of the One who is Lord of all creation. We remain suspicious of either a vision that relocates the kingdom exclusively to the future or one that anticipates a fully realized version through human effort. For some the gospel of the kingdom has become an umbrella for engagement with societal concerns which are unrelated to the primary mission of the church and actually detract from that mission. For others the gospel of the kingdom is dispatched to another era which results in a dichotomized word and deed ministry. For many Christians, the church is the building which services Christians and where Christians find refuge. The homeless are seen from afar or briefly encountered with sporadic mercy missions forays into the city; poverty is kept at arm's length with occasional endeavors to provide food for feeding the hungry; urban blight is seen on the news but never seen up close in neighborhoods which have been abandoned in the name of upward mobility; gang violence is something on the news not something around the corner; and high school drop-out rates of 50 percent are unknown in privileged communities. Sociologists have observed that violent films and rap music "help youths become inured to violence, and, perhaps, death itself. Those residing in some of the most troubled areas typically have witnessed much street violence that has at times resulted in maiming or death."[5] How the

4. Burge, *Whose Land?* 173.
5. Anderson, *Code of the Street*, 135.

church responds to these realities reflects the understanding of its mission. Any response is deficient without the gospel. Any iteration of social justice apart from gospel proclamation compromises the church's mission and turns the church into an instrument for human and political agendas which ultimately fail because they do not address the nature of sin and the need of redemption.

It seems that urban areas struggle more with the relation of the church and kingdom in attempting to address injustice and inequities which often appear more glaring in the city's diversity, density, and depravity. In the city we've gathered for prayer vigils at murder sites, done ride-alongs with the police in bleak neighborhoods as police chaplains, gone door-to-door to install burglar alarms where there had been a rash of burglaries (and used those times to present the gospel), prayed with drug dealers on the corner, fed the homeless at specially planned outreaches, and have seen the gospel at work in lives bringing forgiveness and new life. Urban church planters will need to reflect on how best to be a light in the city, how to engage their communities, and how to express good works, without succumbing to the siren of social activism divorced from the gospel and done simply for the betterment of the human condition. We are all for the betterment of the human condition. The question remains as to the priority of the mission of the church.[6] Some urban pastors advertise themselves as activists and engage in activities which bear little resemblance to or have little to do with the gospel. For one example, I question the benefit of cancelling Sunday worship services to do community gardening. What's wrong with gardening on Saturday with your neighbors? Many churches have long forsaken the gospel and exist only to further social agendas, many of dubious value. Of course, good deeds should flow from the gospel and the church cannot be silent on sin in whatever form it takes.

No one denies the reality of poverty, homelessness, the need for prison reform, and disparities in wealth and opportunity. The questions arise as to how to address these issues and the means to engage them. My answer in short, which for some might appear

---

6. Sexton and Gundry, Review of *Four Views*, 200–201.

simplistic, is that there is a gospel priority in the mission of the church. The gospel addresses ultimate issues, eternal salvation or eternal separation from God. The preaching of the gospel does not remove all societal ills. There will be many good causes crying out for your attention. The good news of the gospel is the main thing. The gospel does, however, transform people's lives, change their relationships and values, and provide a community of believers to come alongside them in their struggles. That does not mean that everyone will be lifted out of poverty or be given equal opportunity in housing and employment, that racism will disappear or that institutions and those who govern will be just. Yet the gospel addresses all facets of life as it addresses sin and Christians become salt and light in their communities and in the institutions where they work. These institutions and communities will not be redeemed. The city will not be redeemed according to some utopian dream. Individuals will be redeemed to live as God's people as citizens of his kingdom and citizens of their community. They are then free to invest their time in multiple causes, perform good deeds and engage in worthwhile activities. Their engagement might very well be encouraged by the church, in some measure supported by the church, but does not demand the church's direct involvement. Their mission or ministry does not become the church's mission.

We thank God that in our personal experience we are already redeemed by the blood of Christ with forgiveness of sins, while knowing that we are not yet completely free from sin and temptation. We have an inheritance promised to us in heaven and in the new creation, but we are still living in a sin-troubled world waiting to be set free (Rom 8:22). We are already saved yet not fully saved, awaiting the redemption of the body (Rom 8:23) and our entrance into the new creation in glorious bodies. We already experience a taste of kingdom living among God's people in the church as the kingdom expression for this age, but do not yet live in complete harmony. We have so much already in Christ and through the gospel but when we look at the world, at crime, violence, child prostitution, human trafficking, drug cartels, dictators, corruption, we see that Christ's kingdom is not yet fully come. In the city, "the drug trade, so dangerous and problematic for local communities and for society, becomes normal happenstance. In destitute inner-city communities, it is in fact becoming increasingly difficult to distinguish poverty from drug involvement."[7] So we pray—"Your kingdom come, your will be done on earth as it is in heaven." Not only do we pray, we endeavor by the word of the gospel and by deed to confront evil as it manifests itself in brokenness and in the torn fabric of society. We confront evil through preaching the gospel and by living out the gospel as it addresses homelessness, poverty, exploitation, injustice, crime-ridden streets, and gang violence as spiritual problems and inimical to God's already inaugurated, not yet consummated reign. His reign has arrived in the person of his Son Jesus Christ who in his earthly ministry invaded the territory of Satan and in his death dealt a decisive blow to the forces of evil. As Wright observes, "we must avoid the arrogance of triumphalism . . . imagining that we can build the kingdom by our own efforts" and "we must reject defeatism . . . which says there's no point in even trying."[8] Carson sagely sums up the issue:

> From a biblical-theological perspective, these challenges, as serious as they are, are reflections of the still deeper problem—our odious alienation from God. If we tackle these problems without tackling what is central, we are merely playing around with symptoms. This is no excuse for Christians not to get involved in these and many other issues. But it is to insist that where we get involved in such issues, many of which are explicitly laid upon us in scripture, we do so from the centre out, beginning with full-orbed gospel proclamation and witness and passion, and then, while acknowledging that no one can do everything, doing our 'significant something' to address the wretched entailments of sin in our world.[9]

---

7. Anderson, *Code of the Street*, 111.
8. Wright, *Surprised by Hope*, 216.
9. Carson, "Biblical Gospel," 83.

There are abuses committed and misguided agendas in the name of the kingdom of God and attached to social justice issues. Churches also risk compromising alliances in the quest for social justice. As Christians, we are more concerned about biblical justice and divine mercy. The justice of God was satisfied by the death of his Son. As a result, God offers mercy to those who believe. As the gospel of God's reign is proclaimed, and as men and women submit themselves to his authority, the already inaugurated, not yet consummated, reign of God is extended. When we preach the gospel of the kingdom as Jesus and the apostles did, we are not preaching something other than the gospel of God's grace. We are warning and inviting sinners to repent and to submit to God's reign in their lives and to experience spiritual transformation which touches on every area of life. We will not bring in the kingdom by our efforts but our efforts bear witness to and reflect the reality of God's inaugurated reign and point to the greater and final fulfillment which only he can and will accomplish.

There is, of course, the well-founded fear that social involvement and activism might detract from preaching the gospel and devolve into a purely social gospel. As we minister in the city, all that we do with the homeless, with drug addicts, with down-and-outers and up-and-outers, we do with the gospel. Several years ago, our church participated in a jazz festival in the community where we had games for children, water ice, and a literature table with Bibles and other literature for free. Once we were told we could no longer provide religious literature, we stopped participating as a church. Now individual Christians can continue to participate as they see fit in many causes. As a church, however, we hold the conviction that the gospel is the response for the city's ills. We will do good in the city even when there may not be an immediate, direct opportunity to witness, and ask God for wisdom. Yet our intention is to always and as much as possible bring the gospel to bear on all issues. Our main interest is not bringing about systemic change in institutions. The church's priority is that every person, man, woman, and child, might hear the good news that Jesus saves. If involvement in the community, if feeding the hungry, if providing literacy training are used to initiate that contact or to further that end, then there is no reason for the church to refrain from engagement. If the church cannot serve the city and its communities with the gospel there is no reason for the church to do what others do, and often do much better, if no hearing is gained for the gospel. In the end, urban church planters will need wisdom to navigate these issues. At the same time, in obedience to Christ, they need to keep first things first and preach the gospel!

Conclusion

YOU MIGHT ASK HOW successful we have been in church planting. I really can't answer that. We've seen God plant churches in many places where we went to minister. In some churches, I was in a lead church planter role. In others, I was in a supportive role or worked with a team. My preference, since I believe in a plurality of elders, would be to always start with a team, at least whenever possible. As far as I know, the churches I've been involved with have all survived my departure and some perhaps have done even better since. But you have probably never heard of these churches. They are not megachurches and I've never been featured on the cover of Time as an influential evangelical leader. Unless your situation is unique, and God works in unusual ways, or if you build on someone else's work, or if you plant an entertainment church to draw crowds and attract Christians from other churches, you will probably have a small to medium-size church. And that's okay. As a matter of fact, once you plant your first church you should pray and plan to plant or support other church plants whether directly from your church or in partnership with other churches.

Our church in Philadelphia is in a challenging neighborhood that would be considered economically disadvantaged. We don't have the luxury of off-street parking so people who drive circle the block until they find a space. Some walk. Some take public transportation. We have an old building to maintain. We are diverse in our make-up and we've discovered that many Christians would rather be in a church with people who are more

CONCLUSION

like them. Many of our people give generously but we still receive outside support to sustain the ministry. Yet we are burdened to help other churches. We do not have the resources to financially pull off church plants by ourselves. So, we partner with other churches and we have provided monthly support for church planters in the city and beyond according to our ability. We support church planting efforts in nations from where many of our church people have immigrated and where we have contacts. Many places no longer need long-term American missionaries to plant churches. Pastoral training is high on our agenda. Several of our elders travel twice a year to train pastors in Cameroon. We try to be wise in determining where to invest with the limited resources at our disposal.

I would be remiss if I didn't mention a faithful Christian couple which has generously supported Grace Church from the beginning. Larry and Nancy had wonderful conversion testimonies of how God brought them together and then saved them. God had blessed them materially and they had a heart for ministry. The first time Nancy called me she said, without a hint of pride, "We have a lot of money. Someone told us you could help us invest in ministry." I assured her I could help. They were humble and unpretentious. After the death of her husband, Nancy remarried. She has continued month after month, year after year to support the ministry. I have told her that, humanly speaking, without her gifts we would not be able to carry out all the ministry we do, especially pastoral training overseas. They were God's gift to the church. Make friends in ministry and for ministry. God may give you a Larry and Nancy.

Urban church planting should not be entered into hastily. It takes time to discern where to go, where to meet, who to work with, and how to feed the family. It takes prayer and patience to make sure husband and wife are really united and see this as God's will for their lives. You will have your share of joys and disappointments. Your church plant might not survive. It might merge with another church. Or it might thrive. We are co-laborers with the Lord Jesus. It is his church. The Lord of the

CONCLUSION

harvest wants you to be faithful, in season, out of season, good times when the ministry thrives, difficult times when you don't know what to do or to whom to turn. In all those moments, you can trust the One who has sacrificed himself for you. He will not spare you all pain. But you will never walk alone.

When we moved back into the city almost ten years ago, someone in our suburban church told me he thought it was a great thing to do in my twilight years. I told him to step out into the parking lot and he would get a taste of someone in their twilight years. Seriously, with age comes a decline in energy, doubt or questions about the next phase of life, and thoughts about investing well whatever time might be left before God's exit strategy. I wish I could say that I've always had an unwavering confidence in the Lord and his will for my life. I would like to say that I have always faithfully fulfilled his charge. But I can't. I can say that God has never wavered. He has never failed. And he shows his unwavering love and his sustaining grace to us his children. I guess I've never gotten over the fact that he saved a high school dropout, a law-breaking drug addict and dealer, and transformed my life. He saved me from a ruined, aimless life and from eternal damnation. Without Christ as Savior my earthly life would've probably ended years ago through overdose or wasted away in prison. After over forty-one years of marriage with the woman I love who is my best friend, almost forty years of ministry, two foreign languages learned, and unimaginable education opportunities, my interest is in passing something on to the next generation. If God calls you to urban church planting you can be sure it will be in some ways more, different, better, or worse than you ever imagined, at different times or at the same time. You may fail to accomplish your purposes. God will never fail to accomplish his. He wants you to remain faithful in your preaching, in loving your family and others, in evangelizing and discipling others. He does not want you to cave to the siren calls of the world or to capitulate to the religious fads and perversions of truth. He does not promise success. He promises his presence. If God has called you to plant an urban church, he will prepare the

Conclusion

way and a people for his name. He will provide and he will give you more than you can handle alone. You may never be one of the great conference speakers or authors. In eternity I don't think it will matter how much human recognition or acclaim you've received. A "well done" from Jesus will be enough!

Bibliography

Anderson, Elijah. *Code of the Street: Decency, Violence, and the Moral Life of the Inner City*. New York: Norton, 1999.

Bergquist, Linda, and Michael D. Crane. Review of *City Shaped Churches: Planting Churches in the Global Era*, by Stephen M. Davis. *Themelios* 44 (April 2019) 199–200.

Burge, Gary M. *Whose Land? Whose Promise?* Cleveland: Pilgrim, 2003.

Carson, D. A. "The Biblical Gospel." In *For Such a Time as This: Perspectives on Evangelicalism, Past, Present and Future*, edited by Steve Brady and Harold Rowdon, 75–85. London: Evangelical Alliance, 1996.

Chapell, Bryan. *Christ-Centered Worship: Letting the Gospel Shape Our Practice*. Grand Rapids: Baker Academic, 2009.

Conn, Harvie M., et al. *The Urban Face of Mission: Ministering the Gospel in a Diverse and Changing World*, edited by Manuel Ortiz and Susan S. Baker. Phillipsburg, NJ: P&R, 2002.

Conn, Harvie M., and Manuel Ortiz. *Urban Ministry: The Kingdom, the City and the People of God*. Downers Grove: Intervarsity, 2010.

France, R. T. *The Gospel of Mark in NIGTC*. Grand Rapids: Eerdmans, 2002.

Guder, Darrell L., ed. *Missional Church: A Vision for the Sending of the Church in North America*. Grand Rapids: Eerdmans, 1998.

Ladd, George Elton. *Presence of the Future: The Eschatology of Biblical Realism*. Grand Rapids: Eerdmans, 1996.

Ortiz, Manuel. "The Church in the City." In *The Urban Face of Mission: Ministering the Gospel in a Diverse and Changing World*, edited by Manuel Ortiz and Susan S. Baker, 43–59. Phillipsburg, NJ: P&R, 2002.

Sexton, Jason S., and Stanley N. Gundry, eds. Review of *Four Views on the Church's Mission*, by Stephen M. Davis. *Missiology* 47.2 (2019) 200–201.

Stetzer, Ed. *Planting Missional Churches*. Nashville: B&H Academic, 2006.

Stott, John R. W. "The Bible in World Evangelization." In *Perspectives on the World Christian Movement: A Reader*, edited by Ralph D. Winter and Steve C. Hawthorne, 31–36. Pasadena: Carey, 1999.

Um, Stephen T., and Justin Buzzard. *Why Cities Matter: To God, the Culture, and the Church*. Wheaton: Crossway, 2013.

Wright, N. T. *Surprised by Hope: Rethinking Heaven, the Resurrection, and the Mission of the Church*. New York: Harper One, 2008.

www.ingramcontent.com/pod-product-compliance
Lightning Source LLC
Chambersburg PA
CBHW051703090426
42736CB00013B/2520